SCIENTIFIC AMERICAN | EDUCATIONAL PUBLISHING

SCIENTIFIC AMERICAN INVESTIGATES CAREERS IN SCIENCE
GENETICIST

BY MEGAN QUICK

Published in 2026 by The Rosen Publishing Group
in association with Scientific American Educational Publishing
2544 Clinton Street, Buffalo NY 14224

Copyright © 2026 Rosen Publishing Group

Library of Congress Cataloging-in-Publication Data
Names: Quick, Megan author
Title: Geneticist / Megan Quick.
Description: Buffalo, New York : Scientific American Educational
    Publishing, an imprint of Rosen Publishing, [2026] | Series: Scientific
    American investigates careers in science | Includes index. | Audience
    term: juvenile | Audience: Grades 4-6 Scientific American Educational
    Publishing, an imprint of Rosen Publishing
Identifiers: LCCN 2024061143 | ISBN 9781725352568 (library binding) | ISBN
    9781725352551 (paperback) | ISBN 9781725352575 (ebook)
Subjects: LCSH: Geneticists–Juvenile literature | Genetics–Vocational
    guidance–Juvenile literature
Classification: LCC QH439 .Q53 2026 | DDC 572.8/6023–dc23/eng/20250214
LC record available at https://lccn.loc.gov/2024061143

Designer: Leslie Taylor
Editor: Megan Quick

Portions of this work were originally authored by Zelda Salt and published as *Be a Geneticist*. All new material in this edition is authored by Megan Quick.

Photo credits: Cover (main) PanuShot/Shutterstock.com; series art (background) jijomathaidesigners/Shutterstock.com; p. 5 PeopleImages.com - Yuri A/Shutterstock.com; p. 7 Designua/Shutterstock.com, (inset) CE Photography/Shutterstock.com; p. 9 matimix/Shutterstock.com; p. 10 Oleg Golovnev/Shutterstock.com; p. 11 Mima Subota/Shutterstock.com; p. 13 PeopleImages.com - Yuri A/Shutterstock.com; p. 14 FOTOGRIN/Shutterstock.com; p. 15 janiecbros/iStockphoto.com; p. 17 (top) PeopleImages.com - Yuri A/Shutterstock.com, (bottom) angellodeco/Shutterstock.com; p. 19 Kazakova Maryia/Shutterstock.com; p. 21 SeniaDm/Shutterstock.com; p. 23 Lopolo/Shutterstock.com; p. 25 kali9/iStockphoto.com; p. 26 wavebreakmedia/Shutterstock.com; p. 27 michaeljung/Shutterstock.com; p. 29 Monkey Business Images/Shutterstock.com.

Some of the images in this book illustrate individuals who are models. The depictions do not imply actual situations or events.

All rights reserved. No part of this book may be reproduced in any form without permission in writing from the publisher, except by a reviewer.

Printed in the United States of America

CPSIA compliance information: Batch #CSSA26. For Further Information contact Rosen Publishing at 1-800-237-9932.

CONTENTS

IT RUNS IN THE FAMILY 4

THE SCIENCE OF GENES 6

DOMINANT AND RECESSIVE GENES 10

GENES AND MEDICINE 12

DNA CLUES 16

ILLUSTRATING GENETICS 18

GREEN GENES 20

UNDERSTANDING BEHAVIOR 22

LOTS TO LEARN 24

AN IMPORTANT CAREER 28

GLOSSARY 30

FOR MORE INFORMATION 31

INDEX 32

Words in the glossary appear in **bold** type the first time they are used in the text.

IT RUNS IN THE FAMILY

Do people tell you that you look just like your mom or dad? Maybe you share their red hair or blue eyes. Or you might wonder why you and your brother or sister don't look very much alike at all. The answer is in your genes!

Genes carry information about a person, including traits. These traits are everything from hair color and height to health conditions and talents, such as being good at music. Genetics is the study of genes and **inherited** traits. Geneticists are scientists who **research** how genes are passed along and how they might change from parent to child.

FUN FACT

DO YOU KNOW HOW MUCH YOU HAVE IN COMMON WITH ANIMALS? HUMANS SHARE 98 PERCENT OF OUR GENES WITH CHIMPANZEES, 85 PERCENT WITH MICE, AND 80 PERCENT WITH COWS. WE ARE EVEN ABOUT 70 PERCENT GENETICALLY RELATED TO WORMS!

Our genes play a big part in what we look like.

THE SCIENCE OF GENES

All living things are made up of cells. Inside those cells are structures called **chromosomes**. Chromosomes are made up of **molecules** called deoxyribonucleic acid, or DNA for short. This is where we find genes, which are small sections of DNA.

Most human cells have 23 pairs of chromosomes. When a baby forms, it starts as a single cell from the mother and one from the father. Each of those cells contains 23 chromosomes. When they join, they form 23 pairs of chromosomes. The cells then divide over and over as the baby grows. Each new cell has a copy of the first 23 pairs of chromosomes.

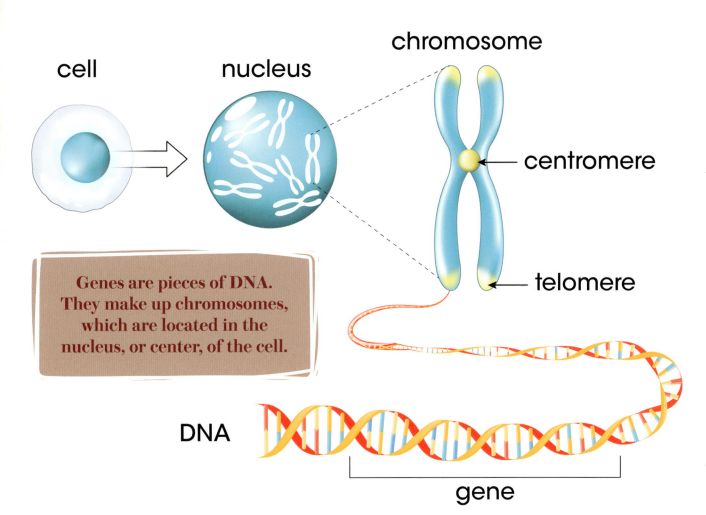

cell → nucleus

chromosome

centromere

telomere

DNA

gene

Genes are pieces of DNA. They make up chromosomes, which are located in the nucleus, or center, of the cell.

FUN FACT

THE 23RD CHROMOSOME IN EACH SET DETERMINES WHETHER A PERSON IS A BOY OR A GIRL. BOYS HAVE ONE X AND ONE Y CHROMOSOME. GIRLS HAVE TWO X CHROMOSOMES.

7

DNA contains tons of information. This includes instructions for making proteins, which make up most of your body. Proteins are found in muscles, bones, blood, and even hair. They help the body grow and work the way it should.

Each gene contains special instructions for making proteins, which affect different parts and functions of the body. As a result, each gene plays a different role and determines a certain trait.

Some DNA is not part of a gene, but its role is to help genes do their job. This DNA gives directions about when, how, and where in the body proteins should be made.

FUN FACT

ONE STRAND OF DNA IS ABOUT 6 FEET (2 M) LONG. IF YOU UNROLLED ALL OF THE DNA IN YOUR BODY, IT WOULD BE LONG ENOUGH TO MAKE 150,000 TRIPS TO THE MOON!

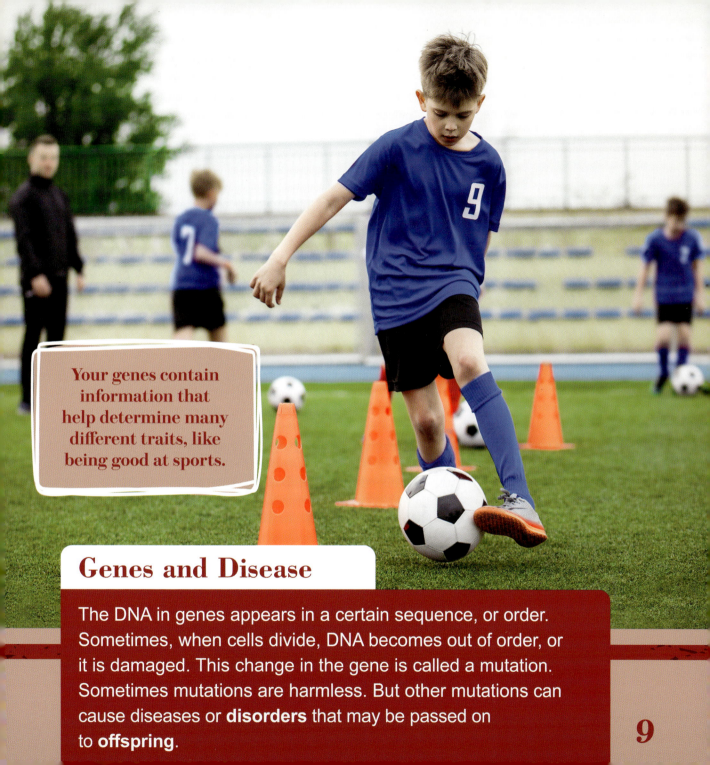

Your genes contain information that help determine many different traits, like being good at sports.

Genes and Disease

The DNA in genes appears in a certain sequence, or order. Sometimes, when cells divide, DNA becomes out of order, or it is damaged. This change in the gene is called a mutation. Sometimes mutations are harmless. But other mutations can cause diseases or **disorders** that may be passed on to **offspring**.

DOMINANT AND RECESSIVE GENES

Each parent passes on a set of genes to their child. If one parent has brown eyes and another has blue, what determines which trait the child will receive? Some genes are dominant, or stronger. Others are recessive, and the trait will only show up if both parents carry the gene.

A Punnett square is an example of geneticists' work. It represents how genes are inherited. Punnett squares show what chance an offspring has of displaying a certain trait. When we pair dominant and recessive traits, the dominant trait will always be the one displayed. When two recessive genes are paired, the recessive trait will be displayed.

Punnet Squares

Each box in these Punnett squares is one of four possible outcomes. Each parent has two different versions of a gene, called alleles. Two alleles— one from each parent— combine to determine a child's eye color.

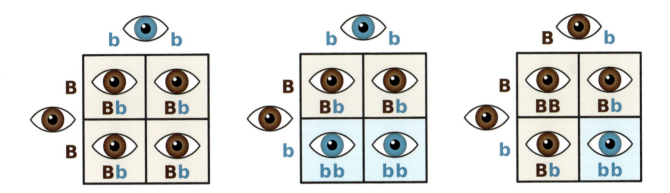

B - DOMINANT BROWN EYE ALLELE

b - RECESSIVE BLUE EYE ALLELE

Where Did That Come From?

Why don't we inherit all of our parents' traits? Parents might carry recessive genes, which may be passed to their child. Sometimes gene changes or mutations occur. And many traits are neither dominant nor recessive. A child has about the same chance of inheriting them or not.

GENES AND MEDICINE

Genetics is a growing field. If you have an interest in medicine as well as helping people, you might want to be a medical geneticist. Medical geneticists treat and **diagnose** people. They manage genetic disorders through medicine and gene therapy. Medical geneticists have medical degrees, because while their work focuses on genetics, they are doctors.

There are many different types of medical geneticists. Genetic pathologists diagnose people with genetic diseases, such as cystic fibrosis and Huntington's disease. Genetic researchers develop knowledge and medicine that doctors use. Genetic counselors help families manage inherited disorders. They support families and advise them on health plans.

A medical geneticist may discuss possible inherited diseases with people who are going to have a baby.

When a person inherits a gene that causes a disease, there might be several ways to treat the disease, including **surgery**. A medical geneticist treats genetic diseases by working directly with genes instead of performing surgery. One fairly new treatment is gene therapy.

Medical geneticists working in gene therapy develop treatments where they replace harmful genes with new genes. This can be done by injecting treatment into the part of the body where the harmful genes are. A geneticist can also "turn off" a disease-causing gene. This may be done by creating a break in the DNA, which stops the genetic information from spreading.

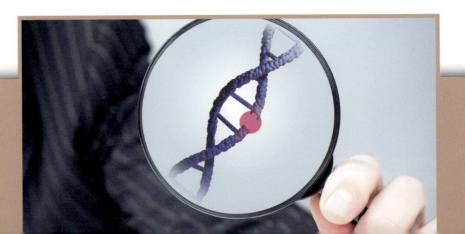

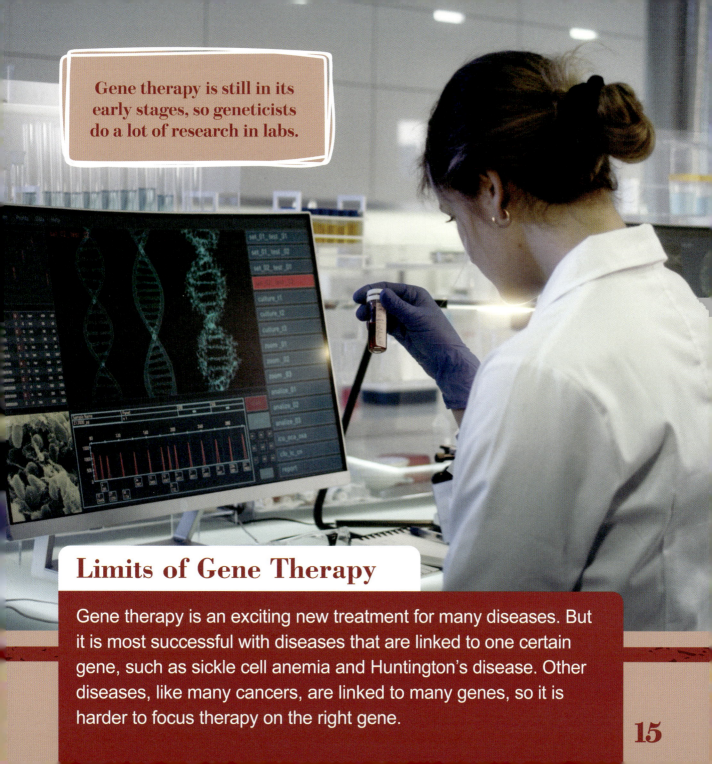

Gene therapy is still in its early stages, so geneticists do a lot of research in labs.

Limits of Gene Therapy

Gene therapy is an exciting new treatment for many diseases. But it is most successful with diseases that are linked to one certain gene, such as sickle cell anemia and Huntington's disease. Other diseases, like many cancers, are linked to many genes, so it is harder to focus therapy on the right gene.

DNA CLUES

Have you ever wanted to help solve crimes? There's an area of genetics for that! Forensic geneticists use their understanding of genes and DNA to help solve crimes using science.

DNA is in every part of a person, including blood and hair. If a **suspect**'s DNA is found at a crime scene, genetics can be used to help identify them. Even years after a crime, a geneticist can match old DNA to new samples when they come in. If someone committed a crime in the past, they could be linked to that crime. Forensic geneticists usually work in a lab, where they study **evidence** from the crime scene.

FUN FACT

FORENSIC GENETICISTS DON'T ONLY USE DNA TO FIND BAD GUYS! THE INNOCENCE PROJECT IS A GROUP THAT FREES PEOPLE WHO WERE WRONGLY PUT IN JAIL. AS OF 2024, THEY HAD FREED 203 PEOPLE USING DNA TESTING.

DNA is collected from a crime scene and then taken to a lab to test.

17

ILLUSTRATING GENETICS

If you have an interest in art as well as genetics, you might consider a career as a medical illustrator. Medical illustrators bring science to life in books and on screen. Their goal is to create medical images that explain complicated information in a clear, visual way. This could include illustrations of the human genome, or all of the DNA found in a cell, and other items related to genetics. They need a good eye for detail!

Medical illustrators may also make videos or 3D images for websites or educational materials. They might work for places such as colleges, hospitals, publishing companies, or law firms.

Cell Structure

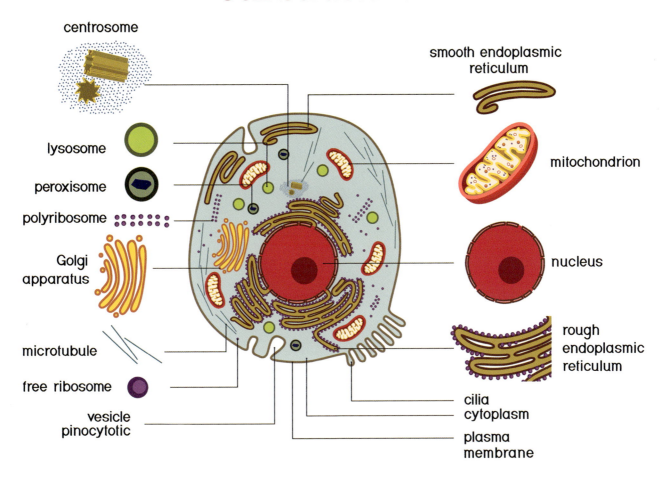

Medical illustrators create detailed images that can help people learn more about a subject. This textbook illustration explains the parts of a cell, including the nucleus.

GREEN GENES

Geneticists do not only focus on human genes. Plant geneticists study the DNA of plants and crops to find ways to improve their traits as well as create new types of plants. They work to create seeds that can better resist disease, need less water to grow, produce more crops, and contain more vitamins and nutrients, which a living thing needs to grow and stay alive.

They study how plants **reproduce** and may crossbreed different plants to create a new variety. These crops are known as genetically modified organisms, or GMOs.

Plant geneticists work in the field of **agriculture**, for the government or food companies. They might also work at universities doing research or teaching.

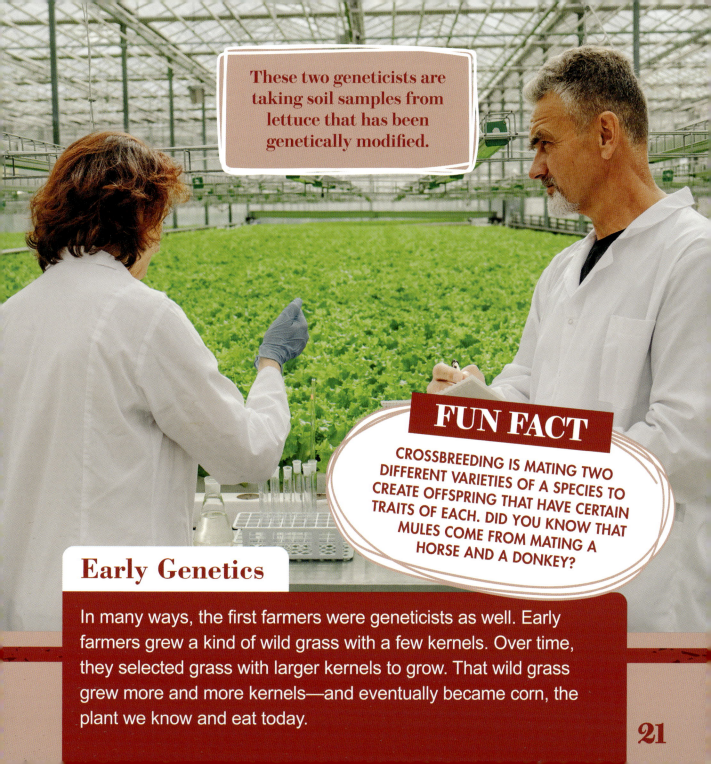

These two geneticists are taking soil samples from lettuce that has been genetically modified.

FUN FACT

CROSSBREEDING IS MATING TWO DIFFERENT VARIETIES OF A SPECIES TO CREATE OFFSPRING THAT HAVE CERTAIN TRAITS OF EACH. DID YOU KNOW THAT MULES COME FROM MATING A HORSE AND A DONKEY?

Early Genetics

In many ways, the first farmers were geneticists as well. Early farmers grew a kind of wild grass with a few kernels. Over time, they selected grass with larger kernels to grow. That wild grass grew more and more kernels—and eventually became corn, the plant we know and eat today.

UNDERSTANDING BEHAVIOR

Genes play a large role in who we are, but they are not the only factor. Our environment, or everything around us, shapes and changes us. Behavioral geneticists try to understand how much of the way we act is caused by genetics and how much is our environment.

A large part of behavioral geneticist research is twin studies. This research looks at what's the same and what's different between twins to figure out how much of their behavior is genetic. A behavioral geneticist might study twins who were adopted by different families. Despite different environments, separated twins may share surprising things in common, such as hobbies or habits.

FUN FACT

IDENTICAL TWINS, OR TWINS WHO ARE BORN FROM A SINGLE EGG THAT DIVIDES, HAVE THE SAME DNA. BUT ONE THING THAT THEY DO NOT SHARE? IDENTICAL TWINS DO NOT HAVE THE SAME FINGERPRINTS.

Geneticists study twins to see how people with the same genes are the same and different. This allows them to learn how environment affects traits.

LOTS TO LEARN

If you are interested in a career as a geneticist, study hard in math and science. When you are in high school, science classes will include biology, chemistry, and physics. Depending on which area you want to focus on, you may want to take classes in ecology, engineering, and computer science as well.

Many of these classes take place in a lab. Students get to spend time completing experiments and talking about their results. This makes for a hands-on learning experience, which is helpful for geneticists-in-training. But that's only the beginning. Geneticists need a lot of training when they finish high school.

Understanding biology, which is the study of life, is an important part of learning about genetics.

25

The amount of education a geneticist needs depends on their area of study. For example, a medical illustrator doesn't need as much school as a medical geneticist. It's possible to get jobs in genetics with a four-year bachelor's degree, but most careers require further education. Most geneticists complete more school after their first four years at college.

Many geneticists will earn a master's degree, or even a doctorate. This might be a doctor of medicine degree (MD) or a doctor of philosophy degree (PhD). Earning a PhD in genetics means someone has reached the highest level of studying in the field. Most geneticists with PhDs do research in labs.

A college degree is needed for most jobs in genetics. A geneticist may earn a degree in biology, chemistry, or genetics.

AN IMPORTANT CAREER

The field of genetics has made important advances that help our understanding of genes and how we inherit traits from our parents. Through the Human Genome Project, for example, scientists mapped out all of the genes in the human body. Knowing the location of genes allows geneticists to target them to make advances in medicine and agriculture. But there's still a great deal more to learn.

By becoming a geneticist, you might be able to prevent the spread of a disease through gene therapy. You could help create a new type of nutrient-rich crop for people who don't have enough healthy food. It's an exciting and important time to be a geneticist.

The work of geneticists allows us to understand how and why traits are passed along from one generation to the next.

Curing Cancer with Whales?

Whales live a long time and are less likely to get cancer than humans. In 2023, scientists discovered a possible reason why. While studying bowhead whales, they found genes with a protein that could repair damaged DNA, which can cause cancer. Now scientists are looking for ways to use this information to help humans.

GLOSSARY

agriculture: The science or job of farming.

chromosome: One of the rod-shaped or threadlike bodies of a cell nucleus that contain all or most of the genes of an organism.

diagnose: To recognize by signs and symptoms.

disorder: An abnormal physical or mental condition.

evidence: Something that helps show or disprove the truth of something.

inherit: To receive by genetic transmission.

molecule: A very small piece of matter.

offspring: The young of a person, animal, or plant.

reproduce: To produce new life of the same kind.

research: Careful study for the purpose of discovering and explaining new knowledge.

surgery: The treatment of disease especially by operations.

suspect: A person thought to have done a crime.

FOR MORE INFORMATION

Books

Harris, Beatrice. *Jobs in Genetic Engineering*. New York, NY: Cavendish Square Publishing, 2024.

Rea, Victoria. *How Do You Look Like You?* Franklin, TN: Flowerpot Press, 2024.

Schwartz, Heather E. *Genetics Breakthroughs*. Rochester, MN: Mayo Clinic Press Kids, 2024.

Websites

American Museum of Natural History
www.amnh.org/explore/ology/genetics
Learn about genetics through fun videos, games, and activities.

Britannica Kids: Genetics
kids.britannica.com/kids/article/genetics/353170
Find out more information about genes, chromosomes, and inherited traits.

Ducksters: Genetics
www.ducksters.com/science/biology/genetics.php
Read interesting facts about genetics and then take a quiz to test your knowledge.

Publisher's note to educators and parents: Our editors have carefully reviewed these websites to ensure that they are suitable for students. Many websites change frequently, however, and we cannot guarantee that a site's future contents will continue to meet our high standards of quality and educational value. Be advised that students should be closely supervised whenever they access the internet.

INDEX

allele, 11

behavioral geneticist, 22

cells, 6, 7, 9, 18, 19

chromosome, 6, 7

diseases, 9, 12, 14, 15, 20, 28

DNA, 6, 7, 8, 9, 14, 16, 17, 18, 19, 20, 23, 29

forensic geneticist, 16

gene therapy, 14, 15, 28

genetic counselors, 12

GMOs, 20

human genome, 18, 28

Human Genome Project, 28

medical geneticist, 12, 13, 14, 26

medical illustrator, 18, 19, 26

mutation, 9, 11

plant geneticist, 20

proteins, 8, 29

Punnett square, 10, 11

school, 24, 26

traits, 4, 8, 9, 10, 11, 20, 21, 23, 28, 29
   dominant, 10, 11
   recessive, 10, 11

twins, 22, 23